ITALIAN WOMEN IN BLACK DRESSES

ESSENTIAL POETS SERIES 116

MARIA MAZZIOTTI GILLAN

ITALIAN WOMEN
IN BLACK DRESSES

GUERNICA

TORONTO·BUFFALO·CHICAGO·LANCASTER (U.K.)

2003

Antonio D'Alfonso, editor
Guernica Editions Inc.
P.O. Box 117, Station P, Toronto (ON), Canada M5S 2S6
2250 Military Road, Tonawanda, N.Y. 14150-6000 U.S.A.

Distributors:
University of Toronto Press Distribution,
5201 Dufferin Street, Toronto, (ON), Canada M3H 5T8

Gazelle Book Services, Falcon House, Queen Square, Lancaster LA1 1RN U.K.

Independent Publishers Group,
814 N. Franklin Street, Chicago, Il. 60610 U.S.A.

Typesetting by Selina.
First edition, first printing, November 2002.
Second printing, June 2003.
Printed in Canada.

Legal Deposit – Second Quarter
National Library of Canada
Library of Congress Catalog Card Number: 2002113454

National Library of Canada Cataloguing in Publication
Gillan, Maria Mazziotti
Italian women in black dresses / Maria Mazziotti Gillan.
(Essential poets series ; 116)
Poems.
ISBN 1-55071-156-3
I. Title. II. Series.
PS3557.I375I83 2002   811'.54   C2002-904807-9

Contents

Acknowledgments

The following poems have been published previously: "Donna Laura," "These Are the Words I Have Said," "When I Was a Young Woman" in *Prairie Schooner,* 2001. "Poem to My Husband of Thirty-three Years" in *Connecticut Review,* Spring 1999. "Something I Always Wanted But Didn't Get" in *Connecticut Review,* Fall 1999. "Since Laura Died" and "A Geography of Stars" in *Connecticut Review,* Fall 2001. "What I Didn't Learn in School" in *Rattle,* 2001. "The Cup," "Song in Praise of Spring," "Return," "The Softness of Snow," "Rainbow Over the Blue Ridge Mountains," "Is This What It's Like?" in *Christian Science Monitor,* 1999, 2000, 2001. "Fourteenth Christmas" in *LIPS* magazine, issue 21. "The Bed," "In the Stacks of the Paterson Public Library," and "Phone Calls" in *LIPS,* Issue 23, September, 2000. "Nonno," in *Corragio* (Women's Press). "Laura, Now That You Are Gone" and "Talking About Underwear," in *Long Shot,* Vol. 24, 2001. "Water Chestnut" and "When I Leave You" in *VIA (Voices in Italian Americana),* Spring 2001 (Vol. 12.10) and Fall 2001 (Vol. 12.2) "The Dodge Silver Hawk" in *SOLO,* 2002. "In the Pages of a Photo Album" in *the new renaissance,* Fall 2000, issue 33. "The Secret I Would Tell," "Shame," and "How to Turn a Phone Call into a Disaster" *Prairie Schooner,* 2002. "My Father Always Bought Used Cars" in *The Southeast Review,* Vol. 21, Number 2, Spring 2002. "Learning to Love Myself," "The Dead Stay with Us" and "The Herald News" in *VIA,* 2002. "Poem to Jennifer" and "My Mother Who Could Ward Off Evil" in *Connecticut Review,* Spring 2003. "This Time Last Year," "Trying Not to Think," "Out the Window," "If I Were a Magic Fixer" and "Growing Pains" *LIPS,* Issue 25, 15, Number 3, Spring 2002.

Black Dresses

I dress now all in black like the old ladies
of my childhood, the old ladies who watched

our movements and reported to our mothers
if we did anything wrong. These women, sitting

on their stoops in their shiny black cotton, their black
stockings rolled down to just below their knees,

their sparse, white hair drawn back into a bun, wisps
of it escaping onto their foreheads.

In the heat of an August afternoon, they sat and fanned
themselves with accordion fans that they held

in their hands and moved back and forth to create
some movement of air. They had big white cotton

handkerchiefs they used to pat away the sweat.
These women kept their eyes on the neighborhood.

They could have told all the secrets of each house,
and on evenings, late, sitting under the grape arbor,

while the men played briscole and the children sat quietly,
They told the secrets whispered among the women,

the secrets they held close to them, these women
who were always there for one another.

When there was illness in the family, they would come
to the door with pots of soup and fresh bread, ready

to help clean the floors or care for the children.
Summer evenings under the grape arbor, the children heard

those stories and they stored them in their hearts,
and the women's whispers and laughter became

the music of a time when the world was small
enough to carry in their hands.

Blessed

Blessed be the moments that remain in our minds years after
they happen, moments like the time when I was sitting
in my mother's lap in the old brown rocker, my sister leaning
against us on the broad arm of the chair, my younger brother
and I caught in the circle of my mother's arm, her body

warm as the wood stove that heated our kitchen, my mother
telling a story about growing up in San Mauro, her voice
soothing and smooth as cream on my skin. My brother's
head rests on my arm as his eyelids flutter and fall against

his cheek, his body going limp with sleep, the four of us
bound together and cradled by my fierce and loving mother.
How warmed we were by her fire, our closeness a warmth
we carry with us even now, more than fifty years later.
When I was leaning over my mother, leaning over the

bed where she was dying, I could hear the stories that
she tried to tell me before she died. When she vomited
black blood into my hand, and died and came back
she told me, "I saw my mother and sisters and they were

in a beautiful garden together. They said it was o.k.
to go now." She held my hand and smiled at me,
a smile so radiant that I thought that she was young
again, the way she was when she rocked us

in her arms. To this day I still hear her
breathing inside me, a place
we will always be together and nothing
to fear, nothing to fear.

Perspectives

When I go back to look at it, when the reporter
takes me back and snaps my picture in front
of our house, the house I lived in until I was eleven,
the two family with the extra family hidden
in the dank cellar where the father got pneumonia

and died, the house seems to have grown smaller in size,
the street, too, small and dirty, soda cans and wrappers
in the gutters. The distance too seems shorter from our
house to Pasquale's corner and Burke's Candy Store
where we got ice cream in coated cardboard containers,

vanilla ice cream packed solid and high over the rim
that we ate with a special wooden spoon on the walk home.
In Ventimiglia's vacant lots we played through summers
chasing butterflies we never caught and playing tag
and hide-and-seek. In that field I learned the only nature

I knew, wild daisies and weeds and black-eyed susans,
the whisper of tall wild grass that hid us if we squatted down,
the freedom of those endless summer days. The field
that was huge and welcoming is covered over now
with asphalt and cement and rows of garages, the earth

plastered over, every inch of it sealed in. The reporter asks
me questions, but my mind is caught in the past, caught
in the scent of Zio Guillermo's garden, the silk tassels
of corn, the dew on the huge tomatoes, the smell of earth
and growing things and Zio Guillermo hiding in the garden
from Zia Concetta's anger. The neighborhood children,

Big Joey, Little Joey, Judy, my sister and brother, gathered
on the back stoop in the summer darkness, telling stories
and smoking punks to keep away the mosquitoes. Often,
in the evenings, my mother would call us inside

and wash us with the stiff washcloths she sewed,
and comb our hair. We'd walk to Aunt Rose's
house to sit under the grape arbor in the evening,
the men playing cards, the wine in short glasses
before them, peach slices gleaming in the red wine.

While the men played cards, we sat near the women
who were sipping espresso and talking, listening
to the stories they told till they forgot we were there,
the stories of people we knew or had never met,
stories that come back to me now, tart and sweet,

a taste of mint and sugar, a drop of espresso
in a big cup of milk. Those moments glow
like junk jewelry I buy in thrift stores.
How can I tell this young reporter
what it was like to grow up here?

Her eyes see it as a slum, ratty and poor;
my eyes remember those moments walking home
from Zia Rosa's in the dark, the world soft
and shiny, the stars still visible in the Paterson sky,
the music of stories and words singing in my head.

Holding my brother's hand, I walk ahead of my mother.
I am in love with the evening, the stars, my brother's
hand, the cracked sidewalk, roses climbing fences
and trellises, the vegetable and flowers the immigrants

planted, the stone birdbaths they built, my skin about to burst
in its sweetness, the stories stored up like treasure
that I would find again and again as I grew older.

The Past

The past is a photo album, a collection of still photographs
pasted on black pages, little silver triangles to hold
the pictures in, only these pictures are ones I never took,
pictures of us under Zia Rosa's grape arbor, the grown-ups
sitting around a large oilcloth-covered table, the women
at one end, talking, and the men playing briscole,
wine in short glasses before them,
peaches gleaming in the red wine.
We watched from the fringes of the group,
the men serious, cigarette smoke rising above
their heads, and the women at the other end
of the table, whispering together about the Riverside
families, their voices soft and happy in the summer air.

The light bulbs strung from the arbor buzzed with insects,
and we, children, listened to the stories our mother's told
to one another, understanding only that they didn't realize
how much we heard. Those evenings, the air heavy
with the perfume of the huge clusters of purple grapes
that grew from the vine, the aroma of corn and tomatoes
from the garden, the contained world where everyone
we loved was together, and today, across the distance
of forty years, I would go back, take a photograph
of those evenings, my father's face jovial, his hooked nose,
his clean clear skin, his love of company and politics,
and my shy mother, still young, sexy in her black
mourning dress, her hair shining under the light
of that dangling bulb, her reserve broken
by the company of other women, and the stories
they told, my brother, sister, and I listening

to their voices and drinking cream soda.

I would capture these moments if I could,
my mother, father, Zio Gianni, Zia Rosa,
Zio Guilliermo, Zia Louisa, all dead now,
the only thing remaining to pass on to my children
is this memory that when I, too, die,
will have vanished forever, as the world I grew
up in has already vanished and not even
a photograph to show what once was.

After School on Ordinary Days

After school on ordinary days we listened
to *The Shadow* and *The Lone Ranger*
as we gathered around the tabletop radio
that was always kept on the china cabinet
built into the wall in that tenement kitchen,
a china cabinet that held no china, except
thick and white and utilitarian,
cups and saucers, poor people's cups
from the 5 & 10 cents store.
My mother was always home
from Ferraro's Coat factory
by the time we walked in the door
after school on ordinary days,
and she'd give us milk with Bosco in it
and cookies she'd made that weekend.
The three of us would crowd around the radio,
listening to the voices that brought a wider world
into our Paterson apartment. Later

we'd have supper at the kitchen table,
the house loud with our arguments
and laughter. After supper on ordinary
days, our homework finished, we'd play
monopoly or gin rummy, the kitchen
warmed by the huge coal stove, the wind
outside rattling the loose old windows,
we inside, tucked in, warm and together,
on ordinary days that we didn't know

until we looked back across a distance
of forty years would glow and shimmer
in memory's flickering light.

Sunday Mornings

Sunday mornings my father bought crumb buns on his way
home from the night shift at Royal Machine Shop. My mother

didn't believe in laziness so she'd get us out of bed at seven
and send us off scrubbed and neat to the nine o'clock

children's mass at Blessed Sacrament Church. We still fasted
then before mass. We'd walk down 2nd Ave and up

the 16th Street hill to the old brick church with its long row
of cement steps and its big carved wooden door

and into the high ceremony of its flickering candles,
the geometry of its vaulted ceilings, the dim,

incense laden interiors, the bruised, bearded face of Jesus
on his cross, the smooth dark wood of the pews. In that

mysterious interior, I was lost in a country that buzzed with
meaning, a place where I could let the solemn organ music

that strained toward the heavens, the fluttery voices
of the choir, fill me. In my head I'd make up songs

and stories while the priest's voice rose and fell
intoning the Mass in his strange and lovely Latin,

chanting and ringing his altar bells. Later,
we'd walk home together. My mother

and father would be in the kitchen where the aroma
of meatballs and tomato sauce pulled us in, my mother

cooking Sunday dinner, the tomato sauce and meatballs
simmering in the pot, the chicken and potatoes ready

to be placed in the oven. On the table, there was always
a white bakery bag of crumb buns. The aroma

of the freshly baked buns mingled with the smell
of my mother's cooking. I picked the huge crumbs

off the top of the buns and ate the bun itself last,
smiling at my father who had been waiting for the smile,

each of us circling around those buns, joking and laughing.
My father would sit reading the Italian paper. We'd play

dominoes or start a game of monopoly while we waited
for my mother to serve dinner. We always ate at noon

on Sunday so we could go out in the afternoon to visit
our aunts and cousins, but Sunday mornings were quiet

and sacred. We'd circle around my mother pestering her
for a meatball, not wanting to wait for twelve

which seemed an eternity away. My mother gave us each
a meatball and tomato sauce in a saucer along with hot

bread with butter. We'd go back to listening to the radio
or playing our games. Do I imagine that the air of that time

seems to shine soft and silken?

My First Room

Had no carpet, instead inexpensive linoleum
that had to be rolled out on the floor

after my father carted it home from the store
in his arms. The room was unheated.

The windows froze over with ice crystals
in elaborate lace patterns all winter.

The loose-fitting windows rattled
and moaned in the wind. It had

no closet, the assumption being
that people poor enough to live

in this room wouldn't own enough clothes
to need a closet. And without electrical outlets

there could be no lamp to soften the rough edges.
My first room had a three-quarter bed

that I shared with my sister Laura. It was gunmetal
gray and ugly like the kind of bed used in institutions.

We had a small bureau with three small drawers.
The room was tiny; there was barely enough room

for the bureau and bed. We had to slide in sideways
to climb into the bed with its white chenille spread.

When I was thirteen, my mother bought a pink-shaded lamp
that clipped onto the headboard. Under the glow of that lamp,

I read *Mill on the Floss, Tess of the D'Urbervilles,*
Jude the Obscure. In those books, I was carried to other

places that caught and held my imagination and taught me
the power of language to make even the darkest place
    beautiful.

Gym Class

When I was still a skinny little kid in PS18,
Mrs. Day, our gym teacher, was very tough

looking and athletic. Her freckled face, deeply tanned
even in winter, didn't smile. She'd stand, her hands

on her hips, shouting commands, her legs
with their hard-looking calves positioned,

ready for battle on that polished wooden floor.
I entered the gym, having dressed cautiously,

trying to use the locker doors as a screen.
I was afraid to look at anyone else and hoped

that no one was looking at me. I'd step into
that blue cotton gym suit that needed to be ironed

every time we had gym. It had elastic around the legs
and pants that ballooned out from the elastic at the waist

to the elastic around the tops of our legs. My gym suit
was passed down from my sister who was chunky and

developed early, the elastic was all stretched out and droopy,
the blue was faded from being washed so much. In winter,

we'd have class inside the gym, some children, sleek
and coordinated and loving the opportunity to run

and jump and show off, and some children, like me,
uncoordinated and bookish, incapable of doing

most of the things Mrs. Day required us to do.
I particularly hated the leather horse

we were supposed to jump over. It seemed
very high to me. Mrs. Day would line us all up.

Each person in turn would run toward the horse
while the others watched. We were supposed

to vault over the horse without tripping
or falling on the other side. Many,

or so it seemed to me, accomplished
this feat with ease. Each time, as I waited

my turn I'd think it looked easy.
I hoped that while watching the others

I'd learn the secret of leaping over the horse.
I'd run toward the horse, make a feeble pass

At vaulting over it. I'd end up standing there
as though I'd run into a wall. "I can't do it,"

I'd say, but Mrs. Day would shout, "Try again."
I'd get about twelve inches off the ground and fall

Back again, unable to get to the other side
Of the horse I'd grown to hate. Everyone

watched. Finally, Mrs. Day would give up
and let me off the hook. Every day

I was confronted with tasks my awkward body
couldn't accomplish. "Climb the rope," Mrs. Day

would shout. My eyes would follow the rope
to the ceiling. I'd try, but these skills were ones

that would elude me my whole life. I was perfect
at missing the ball when I'd try to swing at it. After years

of failing at athletic pursuits, I knew before I began
that I couldn't manage the trick of coordination

that it took to be good at these skills. I wonder if the kids
who weren't good at school, the ones who continually got F

instead of A in their work, felt as hopeless as I did
when confronted by that leather horse, or a baseball

speeding toward me as I held the bat
as far away from me as I could.

Kitchen

We ate in the 17th Street kitchen with its scrubbed
oilcloth, its strong, plain wooden table and chairs,

enough for all of us and for all the aunts and uncles
who joined us at Sunday dinners that my mother cooked

on the big iron coal stove with its polished chrome.
She served dinner on the thick, ugly dishes

from the five and ten cent store that she lifted down
from the glass-fronted cabinet built into the wall, served

the spaghetti and meatballs and bracciola steaming
to the table, and my father poured short glasses of wine

for each adult and water with a drop or two of wine
for each child. We were expected to be silent

in that big kitchen with its tin ceiling while the grown-ups
gossiped and laughed, taking turns, it seemed to me then,

in telling stories, patiently arguing politics, their Italian words
floating around my head, soft as a cashmere

shawl, the music of their words, the way it warms me
even today to hear that softness and the beauty of Italian

fill a room, the language that I taught myself not to use.
I can still see that classroom at Eastside High school.

Mrs. Pennyroyal with her delicate intonations,
looking out at us in sophomore year and telling us

that anyone who spoke another language at home
and thought in that language, would score 100 points lower

on the SAT than those who did not. I was sure
she was speaking to me, that I was the only one, though

looking back now I wonder how many others in that gray
room felt the same flush of shame rise in their cheeks.

How many others learned that day to erase their family's
words and force themselves to think in English, denying

themselves the lilt of their first language, the language
of their hearts. I see us sitting under light of that dangling

bulb in my mother's kitchen, the inexpensive glass shade
unable to soften the light. I see the linoleum clean

and buffed to a shine, though worn through in spots
and ugly, the coal stove crackling, the entire table,

my mother, father, sister, brother, my aunts and uncles
coated by memory in a wash of silver light. Italian words

ring in my head, an unrepentant joy that I reclaim
and hold to my face, as if the words were a rose

and I could put my nose to the flower
and inhale its glorious, unforgettable perfume.

Taking a Risk

When I was eleven, I decided
I needed to be punished
for my sins. If I could
expiate them, I would get everything
my heart desired, and that was a lot.

I went out into the parking area
of the Riverside Presbyterian Church,
and dropped to my bare, scabbed knees
and walked across the stones, gray
and chunky, larger than gravel and pointier.

I'd walk around on my knees, the stones
digging into them, and I'd chant prayers
hoping to transform my life.

Years later, in Portugal, at Our Lady of Fatima
shrine, I saw people walking on their knees
on paving stones. Some of them cheated
and wore foam rubber pads on their knees;
some wrapped handkerchiefs around them.
The tourists stared. The penitents
held their rosaries in their hands,
their eyes lifted toward heaven,

but when I saw them, I was reminded
of my eleven-year-old self, those moments
when I walked on my knees, chanting
"Hail Mary, Full of Grace," and pretending
that I was looking for something I'd lost

in case any of the neighbors were watching.
At eleven I was practical so I only did it
a few times and gave it up when it didn't work.

From this distance, I want to comfort
the child I was and the ghost of that child
who still lives inside me, sharing that common
guilt we carry for sins we cannot name.

Halloween Costumes

When I was twelve and in 7th grade Diane Vanderwende,
one of the few Dutch kids in our class where most of us
were Italian, decided to have a Halloween party
at her house on River Street. Her mother, doll-like

and pretty, looked very American. She made a costume
for Diane, a real costume made from material she bought
at the store. Diane was dressed as a woman in a harem
with a slinky costume with sheer black pants

which ballooned out and were fastened at the ankles
with gold straps. She wore gold and black shoes with bells
on the tip tilted toes and a tight fitting top. Her midriff
was bare. Her bolero jacket covered her breasts and had
filmy black veiling formed into sleeves with gold bands

at the wrists and a slit, so her arms were visible under the veils.
The costume was perfect, Diane looked beautiful with her
creamy magnolia skin, her deep black hair and her big
blue eyes. My mother made a costume for me to wear,

but she couldn't afford to buy material, so she used
old net curtains. I didn't know what it was supposed to be.
I suspect that my mother didn't either.
She fastened the netting in layers at my waist and made a

shawl to cover my shoulders and a scarf for my head
made up of the same faded white net which made my skin
look green-tinged and sickly. "I'm a peasant woman," I said
when someone asked. I wasn't sure what a peasant woman

was supposed to look like. The netting was itchy.
I spent the night feeling awkward and embarrassed.
When Diane's mother offered me a piece of birthday cake,
a store bought confection made with whipped cream,
I, who was thin because I didn't like food,

especially American food, and never tried anything new
if I could help it, said, "No, thank you, I'm allergic to it."
Diane's mother and her aunts laughed and kept repeating,
"I'm allergic to it," as if it were the funniest thing
they had ever heard. Diane took every opportunity

to walk around the room, showing off her exquisite
costume. I huddled in the darkest corner
waiting until it was time to go home.

I Want to Write a Love Poem

I want to write a love poem for the big eyed girl I was in seventh grade and for Joe Rogers and his American good looks, for his eyes, bright and deep as willow pattern china. He always tried to protect me, as though I were fragile and needed his gestures, extravagant as Sir Walters Raleigh's flung cape. He walked me home from school past Warner Piece Dye Works and the weedy cracks in the sidewalk, past Cuccinello's candy store where neither of us could afford to stop.

I want to write a love poem for Joe Rogers who was beaten every night by his drunken father. I'd hear the whoosh of the belt and the harsh slap hit his back. After what seemed like forever, I'd hear him cry out. That cry was what his father waited for, and the belt would cease its terrible arc. Next morning, together we'd retrace our path to the school. We both pretended I didn't know.

I want to write a love poem for Joe Rogers and the way he made me feel, though we never said the word love, never kissed. In my mind he had full and feathered angel's wings that would have protected me from all that was soiled in the world around us.

I want to write a love poem for Joe Rogers who, that year, moved out with his family in the middle of the night and never came back. No one knew where they had gone. I never had a chance to say goodbye. I'd like to tell him how I hope he escaped a father's legacy passed on to him with each drunken slap.

I want to write a love poem for Joe Rogers and thank him for the tenderness he taught me. I want to tell him I hope he found in our shy and whispered conversations comfort for the soreness of his wounds.

Parties

Looking back, I remember three parties
but they really could be the same party

because I was always confused, a half beat behind
everyone else, innocent in some out-of-it way

that made people, even when I was a young woman,
want to protect me. Partially I think it was my big dark eyes,

my wild hair that refused to be anything but the frizzy
hair of someone thoroughly foreign and young.

When I see pictures of Renaissance women, I see myself,
my long thin face, that Mediterranean look.

I was always reading, escaping into the world of books
that seemed so much more beautiful and alive

than the world of 19th Street, with its tilted cement
front porch that went right up to curb and Warner

Piece Dye Works across the street. I remember a party
in 7th grade at Ralphie Corollo's house on 18th Street.

We played spin the bottle. When the bottle pointed toward me,
I was awkward and embarrassed. I went into a corner to kiss

Richie, Nick, or Joe. Most of the time I turned my head
just as they were about to kiss me, and their kiss

landed on my cheek or eyebrow. I had a hard time
figuring out what to do with my nose. If the kiss

did hit its mark on my lips, I didn't know what to do
or what I was supposed to feel. At twelve years old,

I felt nothing, though I wanted to desperately.
I think of last month at the poetry reading

when Gerald Stern, whom I had just introduced,
turned to kiss me and tried to kiss me on the lips,

and I turned away. His kiss landed on my cheek.
He went up to the microphone and said,

"Don't you hate it when you try to kiss a woman
on the lips and she turns away?" he said. I was hurled

back to 7th grade, those kisses in corners, the way
I never know what to do in social situations,

though I am old now and should know. That little
girl in Ralph's living room lives inside me,

awkward and inept; she comes out
just when I think she's finally disappeared.

Magic Circle

My mother drew her magic circle around us, led us inside
where we were always safe. She told us stories,
spinning the thread back between herself and her mother
and her mother's mother and connecting that thread to us
her daughters and teaching us how to connect

the same thread to our daughters and granddaughters,
all those women baking bread and bearing children,
teaching us to love ourselves, love them. The stories,
save our lives, passing the meaning on from one
generation to the next, a silver thread, a silver

thread that strengthens us, all those women,
caught in our hearts, teaching us how to laugh,
how to make our arms into cradles
to hold each other and sing.

My First Date

My first date was with Herman Westfall. I was twelve
years old and in 7th grade. I asked him to a dance at the YM-

YWCA. It was a Sadie Hawkins dance. He said "no."
Not a soft no, but a loud explosive one. He leaped back,

as though I had hit him. Herman Westfall was a skinny
little Dutch boy who went to the Lutheran Church

on Madison Avenue. Later, his family would move out
of Paterson to Wyckoff, a safe, neat, upper-middle-class

suburb to get away from us, the immigrant Italians
who crowded into Paterson and who had no idea why

so many FOR SALE signs went up all around them
as soon as they moved in. I asked Herman

because he seemed the least threatening of all the boys
in our class, certainly not sophisticated as Mikey Russo,

or tough as Joey Calsorre, or street-wise as Richie Serbo.
I was sorry for Herman when Mrs. Elmer hit him

with the ruler in 2nd grade, WHACK! the ruler
would go. Whack! Whack! and I would feel I was being hit

instead. Anyway, I asked him and he said no. He sat behind
me and I turned around fast, his No! a sharp slap on my face.

I spent the rest of the morning with the blackboard
swimming before me. At recess, Judy asked me

what was wrong, and I told her. She rushed off to tell
the other girls. Soon they crowded around me.

I said it didn't matter, but no one believed me. Later,
Herman tapped me on the shoulder and told me

he would take me to the dance. I don't remember
the dance, or the dress I wore, or how

we got to the Y on Broadway, or who picked us up.
I do remember my shame that he had to be forced

to take me. I cringe at my twelve year old self,
too shy to say no back to him, to accept

instead the crumbs the girls in the class forced skinny
Herman Westfall to give, pale, anemic Herman Westfall

with nothing to recommend him but his corn silk-hair.

Cafeteria

In the cafeteria at Eastside High School there was a sour
milk smell that slapped my face when I stepped through

the door. A line of kids circled the room waiting to get
their food. The cafeteria ladies, plump and wearing hair

nets, dolled out macaroni and cheese and hamburgers. I
sat at a table with the others who brought their lunch

from home, pulling out my garlicky-smelling escarole
sandwich, or pizza *chiana* or some other Italian delicacy,

and ate shyly in little bites hoping no one would notice
the sharp tang of garlic in the air. Then the voices and

clanking trays and boys clowning with one another to
get the girls attention rose to a high-pitched roar after

a few minutes, and the cafeteria monitors, teachers
forced to take turns patrolling, blew their whistles.

I usually sat with two or three girls who were
my friends and we would talk and laugh together

quietly. We tried to eat fast and get out. The cafeteria
terrified us. Fights broke out regularly and boys, you

know the kind, loud and teetering on some invisible line
between crazy and just plain brash, would decide

to hound someone, especially someone frightened or
vulnerable. One day three of these boys, they seemed

to be huge to me in retrospect, saw us walking out
of the cafeteria, and one of them in an out of control

manic rage yelled at me, "You're so ugly!
Why don't you get your nose done?" His face screwed up

With disgust, and I cowered away from him, my eyes
filling with tears, his friends laughing, my friends indignantly

walking away from him, telling me not to mind him.
"What a jerk he is!" they said, but I knew that they were

relieved that he had picked on me and not them, all of us,
small and fragile, so unsure, the least breath

could change us forever.

In the Stacks at the Paterson Public Library

When I was fourteen, I asked my father to help me get a job. He called the mayor and asked him for help. My father had worked very hard to get out the vote; so the mayor owed him a favor. When my father said I wanted a job in the Paterson Public Library, the Mayor said, "But that pays only 50 cents an hour." My father told me, and I said I still wanted to work in the library. I loved to read, loved the branch library, loved the feel of a book in my hands. I went off to the Public Library where I was told to speak to Ms. Cherry, Supervisor of Circulation. I went there after school, walked from Eastside High to the imposing white columned library, through the marble hall with its curving stair and bronze statues and oil paintings donated by the wealthy old families of the city. Ms. Cherry gave me a sour look, sniffed, and told me quickly what to do; I knew she wasn't happy that I had been palmed off on her and she let me know she didn't like it.

Another young woman started the same day, a tall, beautiful, light-skinned African-American who came from an upper-middle class family. Her father owned a funeral home. She had expensive clothes and straight hair. We both loved books and we liked to talk to each other in the stacks. She knew Ms. Cherry hated us both, but this girl, her name was Anthea, was more articulate and confident than I was. I was incredibly shy and tongue-tied but she'd answer Ms. Cherry back or give her a look that would shut her up immediately. Then Ms. Cherry would scowl at me and find something wrong with what I'd done. She'd yell, and tears would fill my eyes. "Never let her see you cry," Anthea said. "It just makes her happy."

Despite Ms. Cherry, I liked the job, carrying books up into the stacks on the translucent thick glass stairs. Five floors of stacks lined with books. I'd rush up the stairs and shelve the books so I could read for five or ten minutes. Mostly poetry books by Amy Lowell, Edna St. Vincent Millay, Elenor Wylie, e.e. cummings. Light cascading through the stacks, the transparent floors, and onto the poems that soared inside of me, the words seemed to take wing against everything gray and ordinary in my life.

One day Ms. Cherry accused me of stealing a book by Shakespeare. It was missing from where it belonged. Suddenly, all my outrage at the way she treated me, the disdainful way she always spoke to me, rose up, and shy mouse of a girl, I turned on her, my eyes flashing fire. My voice rose so everyone in the library heard, and I said, "I do not steal books and don't ever accuse me of doing something like that again!" my shoulders flung back, my eyes saying if she didn't take it back I'd slug her. She said "I'm sorry. I'm sorry. Of course you didn't. I don't know what I was thinking," and Anthea, standing behind us, flashed me a huge victory grin.

The Bed I Remember

The metal bed, not the beautiful iron beds
with the handmade quilts that are so popular today,
but the gray metal bed that we had, the one I slept in
with my sister, while we were in that 17th Street apartment
in Paterson, the bed where my sister peed on me
every night, the bed with its clean cotton sheets

that my mother washed in the wringer washer everyday
and hung out in the sun to dry so they always smelled of fresh
air and were so cool against my cheeks, the bed where I read
all the novels I loved with characters far removed
from my 17th Street house and my sister

and the damp cold feel of the wet sheets
when I woke up in the morning and the way
we never talked about it, the wet sheets
or my sister's problem, though after a while
I didn't think about it anymore,

until when I was thirteen and we went to the shore
for the first time, to Long Branch, a boarding house,
with my aunts and grown cousins and my mother washed
the sheets out by hand in the claw-footed tub and hung them

out the window to dry, the sheets a flag that said someone
in that room wet the bed. I was ashamed of the waving
and flapping of the wet sheets in the strong breeze
from the ocean, ashamed in front of the other
city kids who congregated on the driveway to play stickball
and tag in the summer dusk, ashamed for my sister, sixteen

already, and still wetting the bed and the way we never
mentioned it. Just the way today, we pretend we don't see
the cracks in each other's lives, the secrets we both know
but will never tell. My mother trained us to carry our own
burdens, to keep our secrets to ourselves, and we have
carried them until they were so heavy we thought we'd die,

our mouths sealed shut by everything we were afraid to say,
afraid that if we started we'd never stop, as deliberately blind
as we were when those sheets flapped in the Long Branch
wind and we pretended we did not see them.

What I Didn't Learn in School

I didn't learn geometry,
Except for the shortest distance
Between two points
Is a straight line.
The rest was a blur
Through which I stumbled,
Confused and uncertain,
My mind tuning out
When poor bald-headed
Mr. McGinn tried to explain
Geometry to all the Alpha class
Math students who caught on
Right away.

Mr. McGinn was going to fail me
That first semester. I walked up to his desk,
Held out my report card, the marks
All written in neat black fountain-pen ink,
And his head snapped up in shock.
On my report card my marks, 95,
100, 95, 100, 100, 100.
"Is this your report card?" He asked,
And I saw his pen hesitate
While he thought it over.
Slowly, he wrote in a 75.
I went back to my desk, knowing
I didn't deserve to pass,
But knowing too that nothing
Would make me learn geometry,
Not Mr. McGinn with his big, shiny head,

Not the pity in his blue eyes
When he looked at me.
He never called on me again.
I did the homework each night,
Struggling to understand,
And for the first time, I knew
What it was like for those kids
Who always had trouble in school.

I was an Alpha kid, and we were
The brightest kids in the school.
Our classes were held on the third floor,
A symbol that we deserved the top floor.
How humiliating, then, to watch
The other Alpha kids learn
All those angles and lines
Without effort.
I sat, still as a beaten dog,
Tears trembling in my eyes,
While I tried to wrap my mind
Around theorems
But always failed.

Dorothy

Dorothy, you wore pale powder blue that 1950s color
that set off your light blonde hair, every day
a different cashmere sweater set a little pullover
that came to your waist and was covered by a matching
cardigan in pale blue with little mother of pearl buttons.

You wore the sweater unbuttoned, the sweater underneath
showing through, and at your neck, a string of small pearls.
Your hair, so clean and thick, fell to your shoulders, straight
but curled under in a page boy. You were the Class Secretary,

bubbly and popular; you were always with Charlie, the Class
President. I see you standing in the hall with him after classes.
You are leaning against the wall, his handsome face close
to yours. When he smiles my insides shake, but of course,

he sees only you with your thick wool skirt, and bobby socks,
you with your easy laughter, Charlie destined for great
things, and you the most popular girl, destined to be his,

with your straight white teeth, your delicate features,
your big blue eyes. I watched you from a distance,
saw the way you cut a charmed path
through Eastside High School. Voted "Mr. & Mrs. Eastside,"
you smile from our polished yearbook pages. You look

like people who are sure to inherit the earth, and I,
on the sidelines, watch you, conscious of where I am
in relation to you that I cannot even envy you, know nothing
could transform my immigrant face, my unruly dark hair,

my long nose, my clothes that are always all wrong.
I want only to watch the light that shines around you,
to touch, for one moment, a shimmering I can never own.

Bed

When my daughter was about eight years old, I bought her a white four-poster canopy bed, living out some fantasy of little girlhood that was leftover from my childhood when I shared a brown metal bed with my sister. I loved my sister, admired her because she was so beautiful and lively, a daredevil who climbed trees and played baseball and ran off with my cousin Philip and his friends, while I lay on our bed reading novel after novel, and dreaming.

When we were older my mother replaced that brown metal bed with a maple bed from Maiella's furniture store, but the room was still so small, you had to sidle around it side-ways..The bed and dresser matched and it was always so clean, it practically leaped up and shouted, the way those towels on TV do, and the bed, that metal bed that I shared with my sister, was a raft that carried me far away from that lop-sided Paterson house with its big kitchen, its wood-burning stove, the squares of linoleum, the oilcloth covered table, the miniscule bedroom painted with paint that was on sale because the colors were so putrid, Pepto-bismol pink or lemon yellow, and it was in that bedroom that I read *Silas Marner* and *Emma* and *The Way of All Flesh* and *Jane Eyre,* those books that made me fall in love with stories and words. I always loved my sister who let me snuggle my skinny body against hers and let me tag along with her friends when I didn't have any of my own yet I still wanted my daughter to have what I did not – the spacious room, the matched curtains and bed-spread and canopy, the delicate carved spindles on the bed, the warmth of sitting on her bed, reading stories to her, imagining for her a life, easier and more beautiful than my own, not knowing, then, how I'd learn to look back at those years on 19th Street and see them through a scrim of silver light, see them as the treasure I'd try to recreate in poems and stories I'd hand to my daughter trying to give her something more lasting than canopy beds to pass on.

Going to the Movies in the 1950s

When I was still young, movie theaters were opulent palaces,
heavy with maroon velvet draperies and candelabra, ornate
carvings and crystal chandeliers. We went as often
as we could to the Fabian or the Rivoli,
losing ourselves in the flickering world of the screen

where people were always witty and charming, sophisticated,
the women wore long satin gowns and smoked cigarettes
in long holders and the men had pencil-thin moustaches,
wore tuxedos, and were always engaging and debonair.
Often we'd see them dancing, their long, slender bodies

keeping graceful time to the music. In the dark
of the theater, we learned that there were people in the world
whose lives were fur-lined and comfortable, their houses
large and elegant, their expensive cars smelling of leather
and perfume. Strangely, I don't think it mattered to us,

not then, because these people with their affected
accents were so removed from our 17th Street world,
our Italian family, our kitchen table covered in scrubbed
oilcloth and our coal stove, that we regarded them
as foreign creatures inhabiting a world

we knew we couldn't live in since we'd never fit in,
but we could visit it for a while in these movies,
grateful to have seen it, but glad to return
to Main Street and to walk together to Burke's
Ice Cream Parlor, if we had the money, or just
to the bus stop to ride home if we didn't.

Even today, though we rarely go the movie theater anymore,
when I enter a theater and sit in the mysterious dark,
I am pulled into the flickering world
in a way I never am when I'm watching the VCR.
Once we took my mother to the movies when we were
teenagers. My mother objected and complained,

said she didn't have time for such nonsense, sitting straight
as a yardstick in her chair, wearing one of the few better
dresses she owned. We never asked her to go with us again,
because she resisted the idea and acted angry,
but when she was dying at seventy-eight, she asked me

if I remembered the day we went to the movies, the only
movie she ever saw. "It was so nice," she said, and she
smiled. "But, Ma, you said you didn't like it! Oh what do you
know? I was happy to be there with you! It was nice,"
she whispered, and held my hand till she fell asleep.

Learning to Sing

I am in the hallway of the 19th Street house. The front door is a double door. One side is always kept locked, the other side opens when you turn a deadbolt. The door is painted dark brown, a color that is also used for the floor, the banister, and stairs to the upstairs apartment, the door to our apartment. Usually we use the back door into the kitchen, but today I have gone out to get the mail and see a letter for me. I stand in the hallway to open the letter that looks official and is embossed with a return address that says Seton Hall University. The letter is addressed to me.

The letter tells me I have been awarded a full four-year scholarship to Seton Hall University in Paterson, and this scholarship covers four full years of tuition. I shout for my mother, am excited to have won the award. We make so much noise in the hallway that the people upstairs look down to find out what happened.

Suddenly, with my family around me, I realize that I will have to take this scholarship that I won't be going to the University of Virginia, as I had hoped with its colonnades and old brick and ivy. I had imagined it, though I had not been out of Paterson more than three times in my life, and had no idea what the University of Virginia represented, the kind of people who went there, the way I would have been awkward and out of place. At least, I will not have to go to William Paterson College to major in Kindergarten or 1st grade teaching as my mother would like. Instead, I can go to Seton Hall, major in English, dream of becoming a writer. When I announce my ambition, my cousin Joey, the accountant, says it's the most impractical thing he's ever heard.

My mother used to say, "Your fate waits behind the door. You cannot see it, but it is there." In that hallway, behind that brown door, my fate came to me: to stay in Paterson, to go to college a few blocks from Eastside High School, to absorb the feel of the city for four more years, to carry the voice of its people, my people, in my head, to hear their stories, and save them to tell. The voices rise in my head , insistent, wanting to be heard, stories they could never have told , never have found the words to tell them. In my stories, I live these people who are so much a part of my life, their voices caught like music in my mind. I had to cry a long time before I could learn to sing their songs, my own.

My Mother Who Could Ward Off Evil

My lucky dress has disintegrated, the underslip, patched with
tape that won't hold for long, and the fabric begins to tear.
I am afraid to be without it, even tattered as it is, that
superstitious belief that I can be saved by wearing this dress,
the same way I was sure, when I was a little girl
and you pinned a scapula and an evil eye horn
to my undershirt, that these magic charms could protect
me from all harm. For years, I was afraid to go anywhere
without them, even when I graduated from an undershirt
to a bra, but I think that you were connected
to those talismans, you were the rabbit's foot that protected
me from harm, you were the one, the marvel
that kept me warm, the hands that soothed and healed.
In the kitchen where you baked bread
and the aroma filled that apartment, I was safe

from the world outside that you taught me not to trust,
the world where all the universe of evil could get at me
and you, in your homemade apron, you with flour
on your hands, you serving bowls of steaming food,
you canning tomatoes and peaches, you chopping
wood for the stove, you could not protect me,
and in your fear, I learned my own, needing something
like a lucky dress to keep me safe as I walked
through all the dangerous, exciting places my life
would take me, the places where you could not follow.

I carry your memory with me wherever I go, and understand
only now that you wanted the scapula and evil eye horn
to give me courage, so that they would make me brave,

when you could no longer be there waiting for me
in your warm kitchen, your arms open,
your eyes welcoming me home.

My Father Always Bought Used Cars

My father always bought used cars. They usually collapsed into a heap five days after he bought them. He was always having them repaired. One day he went off with a friend to buy another used car. The blue and white Chevy that he had was a disaster; he had to pay to have it taken away. We heard him pull into the driveway in the new used car, and rushed to the window to see, the car, a bright red Dodge, with two doors, a sporty model that looked like a young man's car. My father was sixty-two at the time, already retired from the factory, his leg dragging and weaker than ever. My mother was horrified. "What will people think?" she said in Italian, "A bright red car!" My mother was shy, hated to call attention to herself, thought this red car crass and flamboyant, like waving a flag to say, "Here I am." My mother was angry at my father for buying the red car and went around grumbling for years about it, calling him names under her breath as she cooked and cleaned. Maybe she was afraid that the car would bring envy down on us; I don't know. I do know that she never got into or out of the car without complaining. Everyone in town knew my father. He drove, his hands clutching the wheel, his back stiff, at a maximum speed of ten miles an hour. More often, he kept the speedometer at five miles an hour. He was always in first gear. Our cat got to know when he was coming. My father would inch around the corner from Kingston onto Oak and the cat would come running from wherever he was. My father brought treats for the cat – liver and fish – and the cat knew him and would follow him wherever he went, its tail wagging. My mother, who thought cats were dirty beasts who shouldn't be allowed inside, chased the cat with the broom, cursing him in Italian, when she saw the cat sitting on the sofa. When it saw her coming into the house, the cat would hide and wouldn't come out for hours.

Cheap

Cheap – the clothes I wore when I was in grammar school
and high school, cheap and not quite right.
Imitation blue jeans that weren't blue but black,
so everyone knew they weren't the right kind.

Cheap – the nylon see-through blouse I wore in high school,
white against my sallow skin making me look jaundiced,
sleazy nylon that felt strange and synthetic to the touch,
and the plain white cotton slip underneath
with its fake edging of cheap lace.

Cheap – the dresses we made for graduation from PS18,
white eyelet lace, scratchy and stiff, not soft like expensive
lace. The dresses with their little cap sleeves were tight
over the bodice to the nipped in waist, my sewing ability
so poor that my mother had to undo
every stitch and sew it again.

Cheap – the way the word came back to me when I was sitting
at the party where I had chosen to wear the wrong kind
of clothes, as though some sense of style, of what is right
to wear, is bred into others but left out in me, like the time
I went to the faculty party

at Young Pie's house in suburban KC,
and everyone else was wearing short dresses and jeans
and I wore a floor length cocktail dress,

or the time I read my poems at the Ivy League College
and I chose a dress with big flowers on it when everyone else

was wearing tweed jackets and oxford cloth white shirts
and wool skirts that fell exactly below the knee
and neat little black or brown low heeled pumps and leather
bags I felt cheap and like I'd never learn to be anything else,
all those old cheap clothes still hanging on me,
like another skin, only this one I'd never
shed no matter how long I lived.

So Many Secrets

I've told in my poems secrets
I could never have told to anyone else,
Not face to face, not in person,
Writing things down is always easier,

Though sometimes it's taken me years to say it,
Years to write about something that I did
Or said or didn't do even thirty years ago,

Until I write it down and it loses some of its power
To sting, that bee sting of memory that burns
And burns, only words able to take away
The ache like baking soda and water
And in the end the poem to read
Until the memory of that shameful moment
Of cowardice or guilt is eased,

And we can go forward into our lives,
Leaving that memory behind.
We think of looking at the beautiful faces
Of these young people, the incredible faces,
The girl in the previous session who read her poem
And cried and cried. I know that moment
When we reach the cave
Full of grief and shame and love
From which all poems emerge.

What memory do I have
Of a secret I haven't shared
With anyone, not this white paper

With its neat blue lines,
Not this pen. Then I remember my father

Fired again from another job, and my mother's rage
At him, and of me standing in the doorway
Between them, my mother berating him
For not staying at his previous job,
For listening to his friend
That this new job would be a better one
And it turned out not to be,

So he had to crawl back to his old boss
And ask for his job back and his boss gave it
Back but not before he made him suffer,
Took away all his benefits, erased
Eight years on the job
With one flick of his pen

And my father, at ninety-one,
remembering that day,
His hands and voice shaking.
I remember how angry I was at him
For never having enough money,
For always choosing the wrong thing,
And how ashamed I am now
In his hot little parlor,
His torn plaid blanket
Covering his legs,
His eyes filled with the milky film
Of cataracts, and mine filled with tears.

Winter Dusk

The scythe of winter dusk cuts through the last of the sun
in the courtyard, the trees stripped of all leaves, their bark

black as coal. I remember the coal in the cellar in the house,
the huge coal furnace, the scraping of the shovel

on the cement floor, the marks when the coal was fed
through the furnace's hungry mouth. It was always dark

down in that cellar with its single light bulb hanging on an
electrical cord from a beam and its white-washed walls.

In back of the cellar, way past the furnace, was a wooden
room made of rough planks where my father's wine barrels

were kept and the wine press he used to make the wine from
the huge purple grapes he bought at the Farmer's Market

in Paterson. Leading down to the cellar was an uneven set
of rough cement steps that hugged the backside of the house.

Next to the house, the cracked driveway with the strip
of scraggly grass growing up the middle and the cement

of that driveway crumbling. Is it February that I think
of first in that house, February when even the little

city sun that sifted between the close set houses and the
factories wasn't strong enough to penetrate the bleakness?

Was it really the weather or this time of year? Was it
rather a part of living there, 19th street, gray of neglect,

gray of lives going nowhere, gray of despair, gray of the fine
dust of crumbling cinder blocks, gray of sadness, gray

of the courtyard, with its patio and tree, and the window
of another professor with his lamp glowing in the darkening

night, gray of this courtyard miles removed from that
cement gray, old house gray, where I started out?

When I Was a Young Woman

When I was a young woman, I wore a white rubber girdle
though I only weighed 104 pounds and didn't have an ass

or at least I had a very flat one, but all the young women
I knew wore girdles with snaps attached to hold up

our nylon stockings. The girdle had little holes punched in it
to let it breathe, though actually it didn't breathe very well,

and it was difficult to get off. Now I wonder if that wasn't
the idea, underpants, white cotton, the girdle over them,

the stockings, a slip, a skirt, all those clothes intended
to protect our virginity which of course they never did.

It was a little like my mother's idea that if I was home
by 10 p.m. she had made sure I would remain a virgin,

or like the time, the third date I had with the man
I would later marry, when we pulled up in front of the house

in Dennis' old Plymouth and we sat talking, my back
against the door, while we discussed philosophy

because we thought we were great intellectuals.
My mother rushed out of the house in her robe,

her hair in pink foam curlers, a broom in her hand.
She used the handle to bang on the window and yelled,

"My daughter does not sit in front of the house in a car.
Get inside." Shy and awkward, Dennis leaped out

of the car to open the door for me. He barely said
goodbye before he jumped into the car to run away.

Of course, he did come back. I was so humiliated
I thought I'd never see him again, and of course,

the rubber girdle and the early curfew and all
the other efforts my mother made, didn't work at all.

The Cup

My fingers, raised and rounded, are a cup
holding a universe waiting to be filled
with stars, moon, dark November sky.
Outside the window, the night
is a black cape sprinkled with diamonds,
Inside this white room,
I write on yellow paper,
holding delicately in my mind
my life, fragile as a china cup,
so fine that my fingers show through
as pale blue shadows.

My Mother-in-Law

In the old photograph, my mother-in-law is still young and
slender in her fitted 1940s dress. She is holding Dennis

in her arms; he is six months old, wrapped in a blanket.
In the black and white photo I cannot tell what color

the blanket is, nor what color his hair is or his eyes,
but I can see that my mother-in-law has a firm body;

her hair is dark-colored and neat. She is almost beautiful
and since she is serious in the photo, her buck teeth

don't show. She is standing in the River Edge back yard,
their brand new house behind her. I sense that her life

is full of possibilities. She thinks she will bite into it
as easily as a peach. By the time of her first heart attack

when she is seventy-eight, she can't live alone anymore.
She has to move in with us, something she always vowed

she would never do. In the intervening years she has gained
one hundred pounds and lost it again; her wrinkled face sags

and her body, thin, is covered in loose flesh. After a couple
of years, Alzheimer's sets in. One night at 3 a.m,

I hear the front door slamming closed again and again.
I rush downstairs to find her sitting naked

on the couch, immensely pleased with herself. I hire
a Polish lady to take care of her, after she nearly sets fire

to the house. By the time she dies, seven years later,
she thinks people are coming out of the TV to get us.

She hits Dennis with her walker saying, "You're a bad son,
bad son, bad son!" She slams her rocker into the wall

so hard she makes a big hole in the plaster. Now when
I watch TV in the room I called her room, and look

at the picture of her when she was young, I cannot connect
that young woman with the hopeful face with the old,

raging woman I remember. When I see a picture of myself
at twenty-eight at my brother's wedding, a girl I nearly

don't recognize and look at myself now, I think
how we are all broken in half like this, a jagged line

like the pieces of a puzzle that just won't fit,
our image today in the mirror too much to bear.

Nail Clippings

On my desk, I saw a clipping from a nail. Is it mine?
I'm embarrassed that the person sitting across from me

will think it is mine. I can't keep my eyes off it,
the way I couldn't keep my eyes off the nose ring

that one of my workshop students at St. Mary's Festival
was wearing, when she came to me for her one-on-one

meetings about her work. She had beautiful dark hair
and lovely huge black eyes, but I couldn't stop

looking at that nose ring, couldn't stop wondering
how she was able to blow her nose. So now, sitting

at my new pale gray desk, the nail paring draws me
to it. I've heard of people who stole nail clippings

or hair from a person. I've heard that they're used
in voodoo or black magic to put the whammy

on someone. Maybe that's why all those Victorians
had that morbid fascination with death. Necklaces

with pendants containing hair of the dead,
or that picture I gave to Barbara that I found

in Antonina's shop, a picture of a beautiful
young woman in a high necked Victorian dress,

her shiny hair piled Gibson girl style high on her head,
but if I moved the picture a certain way, the face turned

into a death's head, and her body, a skeleton. I gave it
to Barbara as part of a birthday present because I thought

she'd be interested in it. I didn't realize until she opened it
that she might take it as an indication of her own mortality.

How stupid I am not to have realized how she'd feel about it.
When I see her face, I realize that she thinks I did it on

purpose, instead of out of stupidity. I remember a story
I heard once about a woman who saved her bodily refuse

in shoeboxes in her closet. I always had this image
of those boxes stacked up on the shelf in a closet.

Imagine someone's surprise when they open
one of those boxes? Someone told me this story

before I got married. On our honeymoon I was nervous
around my husband whom I didn't know very well,

though I loved him, or the person I thought he was.
I went into the bathroom to take a shower. I stepped

into the shower and, when my new husband walked in,
I screamed. "You scared me." It was a long time

before he came into the bathroom with me.
How careful we are of our bodies, fearing loss and afraid

of giving things away. We guard our hearts the same way.
My mother always said, "The more I gave away, the more

I had to give." I try to live like that. I don't want to be one
of those people who are so afraid of losing something,

they store themselves in shoe boxes so that, when they finally
decide to give something of themselves away,

they find only dried up and desiccated lumps, and not
the treasure they first stored so carefully away.

Poem to John

I

You call me more often now,
ask me to come down to visit
and sound as though you mean it.
I used to feel you didn't know what to say to me
and it made me so sad. The long silence
that I'd try to fill with chattering words scattered
in the air, meaningless as ticker tape,
I'd say something and you'd sigh
and answer me, your voice heavy with resistance,
and I'd hang up the phone and cry
because you, whose hand I held as we crossed the street,
you on whose bed I sat until you fell asleep,
you who used to talk to me, closed up against me
as though I were your enemy, and you begrudged every
    reluctant word.

Now you call me and I feel that you have something you need
to say, though you don't quite get to it.
Maybe it helps to hear my voice as it helps me to hear yours,
Maybe you are starting to know that your children,
who cling to you now that they are small,
will move away from you.
You, too, will be the person on the other end of the line
while your children leave those huge pauses in the empty air,
your children, who breathe when you breathe,
who fall asleep in your arms,
who trust you above all others,
one day your children will be lost to you.

II

I sigh when the phone rings. When I pick it up out of it's tan cradle, it is your voice I hear, deep-timbered and heavy with grief. "What is it, John?" I ask, as though you would actually tell me what it is that drags your voice down and fills it with sorrow. "I'm just tired, Ma," you say. I remember you as a little boy, bent over your model tanks and figures, your tongue clasped between your teeth, your whole body concentrating on painting the miniature faces on the figure that will sit in the seat of this tank. Every knife in the house burned from being held to the flame so you could cut and shape the models. You were always self-contained. Spent hours in your room with the heat turned up high, your books piled around your bed, track shoes, and shirts heaped in a corner. I should have known then how you would move away from me, how necessary is this severing and reshaping of our lives. The burned knife of distance changes what we are, mother and son, a phone wire the only tentative cord left between us. Words that offer comfort stuck like a fishbone in my throat. I would give anything to erase the sorrow from your voice. I say: "Take Care. Are you taking your vitamins? Are you eating?"

III

I remember when I sat on your bed
And we'd talk, how you needed
To have me there.

A huge distance opens between us,
Not only of highway and town,
But like the bowl formed by the Catskills
In which fog and mist drift
So that everything that has grown familiar
Is suddenly altered.

I thought I would always know you,
Recognize you anywhere no matter
How much time had passed,
But all my certainties disintegrate
As we struggle to find the ease
We once had with each other,
The words that floated between us,
Free as balloons.

You answer my questions
With *yes* or *no*, your secrets hidden
In the heavy timbre of your voice,
A grief I hear running like a cord
Through everything you say,

And I, who would do anything
To make you happy, am helpless
Before your silence, cannot find you
Through this fog that ripples
Between us, the way you recede from me
Until I am afraid a day will come

When I won't remember your face
Or the feel of your high cheekbones
Under my hand.

Window

In my third floor room
I am floating
above
this small city
lost
beneath outer vastness.
The endless mountains
are dark charcoal smudges
against the gray sky,

and trees, bare
of leaves, sweep
the clouds like brooms.

Rainbow Over the Blue Ridge Mountains

All day the rain has been rattling its tin shield
against the roof, but now, the noise stilled,
I look out the window and am surprised
by a rainbow over the Blue Ridge Mountains,
in the distance. a huge arc of pink and yellow
and green, amazing and exquisite.

How rushed my life has been,
how fortunate to have this week
to return to the natural world again
and to listen to the first bird
chirping after rain.

Return

I ride route 17 West, and the mountains lift
And circle the road, mountains in front of me
And the curve of others to the right and left,

The evergreens dark feathers brush the sky,
And the trees on the hills, bereft of leaves,
Stand stiff and straight as pencil strokes,
Close together and pointing skyward,

So perfect and symmetrical the lines
They could be an artist's rendition
Of winter mountains.

I try to make a picture of them
In my mind, black pencil strokes
Separated by white snow.

Song in Praise of Spring

I fill the round blue bowl
of morning with silence
broken only
by the soft silver speech of birds
in the dogwood's bare branches.
Under the radiant veil
of this spring sky.
I imagine
the stars shining.

Elvis Presley Is Alive and Well on Lincoln Avenue in Fair Lawn, New Jersey

I am driving down Lincoln Avenue in my little red Honda when I see Elvis Presley at the window of a boxy two family house, with two porches stacked one on top of the other. In the window that looks out on the first floor porch, Elvis Presley sits, his face in profile. There is a light behind him. Even as evening falls in on us, he is clearly outlined. The next time I pass that house, I look for him. This time, in addition to the Elvis in the window, there's a big plaster record and another Elvis, sitting in a chair on the porch. Each day when I pass the house, there's a new addition until the porch has a sitting Elvis, a plastic guitar, a cardboard cutout of a pink Cadillac, a standing Elvis, and an Elvis, knees bent, pelvis thrust out in that Elvis stance, that way of pushing out his hips that shocked America and made teenagers love him. One day when I pass the house, everything is gone save one torn shade: no Elvis at the window, no sitting Elvis on the porch, no pink Cadillac, no record, no standing Elvis, no Elvis in his pelvic rock.

Where did they go to, these people so caught in another era, they who spent this much thought on building a shrine to Elvis, that fire that burned and flared across the American sky forty years ago? Each place they move, imagine them carting all the fake Elvis dummies and cardboard cutouts, filling their lives with Elvis, raising Elvis from the dead, pulling on his skin, driving all the girls to a frenzy with their songs.

The Herald News Calls Paterson
That "Gritty City"

When I leave Passaic County Community College at dusk,
the sky is the most amazing color – deep violet and luminous,
like an old woman who smiling suddenly looks young.
The courthouse dome is outlined against the sky,
the rococo arches of the old post office,
the clock tower of the new federal building,
starkly simple, and the clock tower of city hall,
ornate and elegant.

I love the voice of this city, the eyes
of its people, the whooshing sound of the Great Falls,
the old mill that has become a museum,
its brick work shining in sunlight.

I see the old men sleeping in the dumpster,
the prostitute resting against the walls of St. Paul's
Church, the empty crack vials
in the gutter, the transvestites on the corner,
but, under the gritty surface, a fresh energy rises,
and it is the heart of the city –
it beats in the shinny copper of the fountain
in Cianci Street park, in the old men in the Roma Club,
shrewd and wary, squinting against cigarette smoke,
playing Italian card games and drinking espresso.

It bears in the chests of the new immigrants –
Iranians and Colombians, Cubans and Syrians
Dominicans and Indians, carting their hopes to this city
and dreaming, and in the young men with the gangsta pants,

their underwear showing, and in the bravado
of the girl with the braids and the yellow barrettes
and her starched dress and in the little boy
with his torn sneakers and his jeans jacket
and the handsome clean lines of his face.
I sing this song for them, for all of them,
the saved and the lost, the ones who will survive
and the ones who will not. I sing for the Jamaican family
and their new restaurant and their hard work
and the young Cuban woman who wants to make money
from her poetry, and for those who will find
the city's heart beating under grit
and who will hear its music
and sing along.

The Great Escape

The recruiters for the army/navy/air force
sit behind plain wooden tables.
covered with leaflets on the service,
an officer pictured, bright-eyed and clean,
all his brass buttons shining.

The recruiters, white and clean-shaven,
their close-cropped light hair,
their eyes blue as marbles, stand out in this lobby
at Passaic County College in Paterson, New Jersey,
filled with young black/brown skin and voices in ghetto slang,
and Puerto Rican women in elastic, day-glo pants,
and slender Latino men with clipped moustaches,
and dapper smiles. Out of the crowd of moving,
circulating students, first Juan Garcia, then Kevin Clark,
drifts over to the recruiters.

I hear the sales pitch on how the service gives you a chance
to learn a trade and to have a career, and when you get out,
they even give you a scholarship to college,
Kevin's face turns hopeful, the path
to a better life opening in his mind like a highway
out of this city and the only life he's known,
and Juan listens and he, too, believes.

They drift back to the group. Others replace them.
All day the recruiters talk and talk till finally
at nightfall Jose Jemenez and Khemi Freeman
and George McKay and Keisha Lynette return
to the tables, sign their names to long, complicated forms

that they don't comprehend, the path out of the city
smooth as greased metal.

After Broadway,
after the Alexander Hamilton Welfare Hotel,
after the graffiti on the walls,
after the pimp strutting his four women,
after the garbage in the gutters,
after the screaming woman,
this offer, the brass buttons
on the suit of the army lieutenant,
his polished shoes, and the Air Force
corporal, sharp in her blue uniform and neat,
shining hair, seem to hold out golden keys

to Jose Jemenez, Khemi Freeman,
George McKay, Keisha Lynette,
that they hope will set them free.

On T.V. ten days after the outbreak
of the war, the cameraman
takes a picture of some young people
waiting in Saudi Arabia for the fighting
to begin. The camera scans
the untried, untouched faces of the soldiers.
"We've been waiting so long,
Mason Brown says, I just want it
to start," meaning the fighting,
the tanks massing at the border,
the ground troops waiting.
"This is where I want to be," he says.

Noise

The noisiest place I remember is the Passaic County Jail where they took our Leadership Paterson group on a tour, pushing us ahead in front of the women and children waiting to see their husbands or boyfriends. They let them go inside one at a time, so even when I pass the jail at midnight, women and children are waiting in winter cold and summer heat. We were herded inside. The sheriff was proud of his jail, which was built to house 1200 prisoners but holds 2800. Cells for two hold six prisoners, two sleeping under the bottom bunk on a mat on the floor. He is proud of the fact that the state pays him forty-eight dollars a day to feed prisoners and he only spends twenty-four dollars. He does not return the rest; instead, he operates the jail at a profit. Its inmates are mostly Hispanic and Black. They are squeezed into day rooms too small for that many men. The noise level is so high it feels as if my ear drums will burst: men shouting, playing cards, the TV blaring, radios playing. The hot smell of too many bodies mingles with the noise. I imagine a circle of hell exactly like this place and I wonder how they keep from going mad. I want to get out, to get away from the crew cut and the blue eyes of the sheriff, his self-satisfied smile, and the horrible concert of sound that follows us out of the jail and all the way home.

What I Do Is

Leave dishes in the sink

Look my name up in the Internet and feel happy
Because there are ninety-nine references to me
In one search engine alone

Sleep a lot

Sit on the couch and go through a pile of papers
That never seems to get smaller

Go to the post office and the bank

Collect the mail

Do two minutes worth of anemic exercise

Hear Dennis's shuffling feet in the kitchen

Look through more papers, which I'm sure
Are multiplying like some wild virus
Look at my treadmill, which sits, unused
And stares accusingly at me

Listen to the teapot's whistle

Talk to my daughter on the phone

Stop myself from calling my son
Since I'm afraid of annoying my daughter-in-law

Go to the red, white, and blue thrift shop
To pretend I'm exercising

Give advice to my children and friends, advice
They didn't ask for and don't want

Screen my phone calls

Stall calling people I should call but don't want to

Have dreams in which all the people who are long since
Dead speak to me.

Breathing

When you were still full of the work that filled
your day and evening, when you couldn't sit idle,

even after the evening meal was cooked and the dishes
washed and the kitchen cleaned, after the final chores

of the day were finished, you'd sit in the brown chair
in your little parlor, Dad in his recliner next to you,

the television on, and you, crocheting at amazing
speed, turning out so many afghans that all the children

and the grandchildren have two or three apiece. When
we went to the big bin behind the Bunker Hill rug factory

to pick out the discarded rolls of yarn, you were happy
to have so much yarn, free for the taking. You told me then

that your mother always visited you in the night to bring
you news, and you promised you'd visit me too. I wonder now

that you are eight years dead, now that they boxed you up
in the Mausoleum drawer where I never visit you

because I cannot think of you closed in that steel cabinet,
closed away from the earth you loved. You sold your

cemetery plots because you were afraid we wouldn't take care
of your graves. I cannot think of you, who were always moving,

forced to lie in that one narrow space. I was with you
when you died. I saw your eyes turn opaque and knew

that you were gone, only your body left on that table.
I remember that you told me, when even my doctor

brother thought you were dead, that you saw your mother
and sisters and it was so beautiful there in that place

filled with flowers and light. I want to think that you aren't
stuck in that drawer at Holy Angels Cemetery, but instead

in that heaven of light, walking those paths with your mother
and sisters. I think of how your mother visited you

all those years after she died, and I have waited for you,
hoped to feel your weight at the edge of my bed, hoped

to see you standing in the doorway coming toward me yet,
when I hear your words in my mouth, I know you are with me.

Sometimes I Forget That You're Dead

Papa, sometimes I forget that you're dead.
I start to drive toward your house, and remember.

You've been gone now nearly a year.
Your house emptied by strangers

who went through your closets and sold off
the bits and pieces of your life.

After visiting you every day for the nine years,
I could not bear to go into your house

and clean it out, so I hired a couple to hold
an estate sale. When the sale was over,

your house denuded, only a few torn scraps
of paper and knick-knacks were left.

Old material and magazines were tossed
in tangled and dusty lumps,

I thought about how Mom would have hated
the shame of this neglect,

she worked so many years to keep the house spotless.
Before you died, you wanted your life to be over,

caught as your were in a world bounded by your bed
and wheelchair, all your friends long since dead,

only me to visit you each day. At the end
you stopped speaking, even lost interest in politics,

sighed away the heaviness of your days. Your eyes
no longer lit up when you saw me, and then,

you were gone. You decided enough,
you turned over and stopped breathing.

I forget you are dead, your house emptied
and sold. I tucked a deck of cards in your coffin

because I know how you'd missed the endless card games
you played with your friends. They were glad

to see you. Papa, I hope that you are sitting
under some grape arbor, your friends

around you, every day a perfect fall day,
the sun warm as my hand on your face,

who am here, thinking of you.

This Leaf

On this country road I see the leaf, and its wide hand, its splayed fingers seem to reach out to me. I feel compelled to pick it up and carry it with me. It is maple syrup brown, with a center stem that ends in a foot with three separate toes like the foot of a chicken, at least, I think chickens have three toes, although my knowledge of country life is extremely limited. I haven't seen a chicken's foot in more than forty years. I do remember going to the chicken man on River Street with my mother, rows of caged chickens, squeaking and squawking the floor covered with sawdust and chicken feathers, the smell of fresh blood, my mother and all the other Italian ladies buying their fresh chickens and I stood with my mother while she picked out the bird she wanted, and the chicken man plucked it out of its cage and went into the back and wrung its neck or chopped off its head or both, I'm not sure. I was so young. There was a lot I missed. What I do remember is the noise and bustle of the place, the way the women's faces looked as they chattered with each other, my mother, going about the serious business of life, was self-contained, her feelings carefully hidden behind her eyes, her face brown as the underside of this leaf, its lines and tributaries, a complex map to a country she preferred to keep to herself, fearing the scissored tongues of the Riverside gossips. When I turn the leaf over, the sunshine on it lights it up, the way mother's face lit up once we were back in the 17th Street apartment, and she looked at me for a moment, before she started bustling around that kitchen, preparing the chicken to be cooked by burning off the feathers on the stove. Practical and no nonsense, my mother loved us fiercely, protectively, but she could be tough and strong. She taught us by what she did; to rely on each other and the family.

"Friends," she said, "eh, friends, they only stay around when things are good." Maybe that's why this leaf reminds me of her; the way she was when she was dying, like this leaf, perky and on the ground, even though it's January and should have crumbled to pieces months ago.

I Don't Know

I don't know what it is I want or how
I managed to make this room look

Like it had been in a tornado, blankets,
Pillows, books, papers, bags full of junk,

My decrepit couch – all the rubble of my life
Scattered and messy. My mother is in the room

With me, though she's been dead for ten years.
She's telling me what a slob I am, and why

Can't I learn to be neat and to put things away?
I don't know why in two minutes I can take

A neat room, and even when I'm trying to be careful,
I can turn it into a disaster. I don't know how

To change myself into the daughter my mother wanted,
More like my own perfect daughter who cleaned out

My entire garage, filled to the brim with paper and books
And trash, so that now it looks better than my entire house,

My beautiful daughter who worked hard and lifted
So many heavy boxes until one box was too much,

A box, "not even that big," she says, and she heard something
Snap. She had to sit down, then, in such pain that tears were

Running down her face when I found her. She hasn't been
Able to move without pain since then, despite the Tylox

My brother prescribes which should knock out any pain,
But doesn't seem to touch this one. I don't know why

It seems to have skipped a generation – the way my daughter
Is willing to work for hours at a stretch without stopping,

The way she thinks she can do anything, just like my mother
Who would come into my house, waving her arms wildly

Over her head, and shout, "What did I do wrong?
What did I do? Wrong? Look at this mess!"

She'd start cleaning up and cursing all the things
I didn't know how to do, muttering to herself

While she cleaned furiously. One day
when I told her to get out, because she was

Annoying me, she said I could live the way I wanted,
But she'd never come back. Today, watching my daughter

Who carries my mother's efficient genes, my daughter
I always depend on more than any mother should,

I would call my mother back from the dead, ask her to help
Me clean up the mess. I can almost see her sturdy body,

Moving like a dervish through my rooms till they are clean
And neat. I promise, if she'd only come back, this time

To say thank you, and try to explain
How much I didn't know, and the way now,

Even after all this time, I still need her.

The Story of My Day

I get up at 6 a.m., drive all the way to Trenton
for a meeting where I am held captive for five hours

in a crowded room, drive two hours back to my house
and get right back into the car, after picking up

my books and poems, drive down Route 4
over the George Washington Bridge onto

the Westside Highway and down to 12th Street
and zigzag toward the eastside, squeezing past

parked trucks and screeching cabs and, finally,
head toward the lower east side where I arrive

by 5 p.m. though my reading is not until 7.
The neighborhood is seedy and rundown.

Across the street a huge project sits bleak
and hopeless. I'm afraid to get out of my car,

fearing it will be stolen. I park my car and wait
until it is legal to park at the meter. I drop in four

quarters for an hour and go into the Bodega
where I buy my dinner, a bottle of water

and a bag of barbecued potato chips, and where
the man behind the counter calls me *mami*

and is nice to me as he argues with one
of his customers who refuses to pay for a bag

of chips, saying they were free. By the time I get
back to the car, only fifteen minutes have passed,

so I read over my poems and munch on the potato
chips and drink the water, though the potato chips

leave my face and lips and teeth orange, and I use
a Purell Sanitizing Hand towel that my daughter bought

for me to keep in my car, and I try to clean up my face
and teeth, hoping that I got it all and that people

in the store haven't spotted me scarfing down
potato chips. It is still too early to go inside,

and this is the way I spend my day.

In My Family

In my family we're all tenacious, decide what we want and go after it.

We work hard, moving forward,when we're exhausted, and think we can't move one inch more. I wonder if it's in the genes, this need to finish everything we start, this belief that hard work and perseverance will get us through. My sister kept going to work for months after she had seizures and couldn't walk. Her live-in aide took her to work in a wheelchair, pushing her down the road, because the sidewalks in Hawthorne aren't handicapped accessible.

My father had a degenerative disease of the spine. He dragged one paralyzed leg behind him wherever he went, and went he did, driving until he was eighty-seven years old, cloth around the pedals of the car so he could reach the brake, one shoe built up to compensate for the unevenness of his legs, driving to his friends' houses to play cards and visit, driving to the courthouse in Paterson to file a petition for his friends or register the legal papers he drew up, his body failing him, but his mind sharp and willing him on.

My son John wants to think he is not like us. I hear how even at thirty-two he takes responsibility for his life, how he gets up at 5 a.m., so he can be at his office by 5:30, how he handles the complex legal problems of a large corporation, working straight through till he returns at 6 p.m. to help with the children and to deal with the house, the yard, repairs. He takes everything seriously. I love the way John carries his son in his arms, the child running to him for comfort and the way they speak to each other without words. I know that even my son, who wants to think he is not like our family, is driven as we are to keep on going, no matter what.

These are the things my mother taught us by example, my mother who tripped over our skates when we were children and got up and walked the twelve blocks to Ferraro Coat Factory on River Street. She worked until noon, walked back home to make our lunches, and then walked back to work. Only after she came home at 3:30, so she could be there when we got home from school, did she collapse into a chair unable to move. When she came back from the hospital clinic with a cast on her leg, fourteen bones in her foot broken, she had to rest her leg on a stool. That was one of the few times in her life that I saw her cry, not because of the pain, but because she couldn't do the work she told herself she had to do.

Doris Day

Your movies always ended with marriage,
promising life lived happily ever after.
Rock Hudson was always your groom,
the handsome man who chased you
through numerous misunderstandings
until you agreed to be his forever.
In The Rivoli or The Fabian Theater,

we watched you, longed
with all our sixteen year old hearts
for your life: the luxurious white
peignoir, the roses on the breakfast tray,
the absence of any real tragedy,
a world without dead children

or atrophied love, your life lived
on the surface where everything
you ever wanted was finally yours.
We followed you adoringly down
that red-carpeted aisle, the white
wedding gown, the tiered wedding cake,

the limousine, the handsome groom,
and were shocked, then, to find
it was only a dream after all,
a celluloid fantasy we wanted to live out.
We tried for years not to know
That love often led to grief and sorrow,

that a house can be empty even
when it is full of people, that loss
is a burden we must carry alone.
Oh perky Doris, even you must
have suspected that what you
were selling was counterfeit.
Where are you now, Doris Day?
Were you as fooled as we were
by those Technicolor moments,
some part of you wanting to believe
that your life, too, could be easy
and smooth, all scented cream
and satin, and that like Sleeping Beauty

you needed a man to wake you?
Are you longing now for sleep
into which you can escape
the monotony of marriage
lived in black and white?

Nancy Drew, I Love You

Nancy Drew, at eleven, I loved you, read every one
of your books, over and over. You became
the best friend I didn't have that year.

I imagined following you into caves and woods,
climbing rope ladders, exploring secret passages
in old mansions. In my mind, your flashlight, large

as a whale's eye, illuminated mysteries.
Stepping into that circle of light, I left behind
the skinny Italian girl, mute with shyness,
timid about roller skating on slippery slate
sidewalks, too afraid of water

to ever learn to swim, frightened
by the speed of bicycles and roller coasters,
afraid of teachers who looked at me
and found me lacking, my black hair
kinking out into a tent around my head,
my huge and sorrowful eyes staring through them.

Gladly, I would have become you, pulled on
your white skin like a silk dress. I pretended
I could be you, outspoken and gregarious,
brave and wily. I imagined you would want me

to be your friend. I imagined
I could go into our dank immigrant cellar
with its coal stove and mouse traps
and its smell of fermenting grapes,

and behind the huge wine barrels,
I would find a secret room like the kind

you always found in your books. Nancy,
I wanted to be you, despite all the evidence
that nothing could transform me,

I, who stared at the rope in gym
as though it were alive, and struggled
to climb up one foot before I fell

to the polished floor. I knew you had
so many things I wanted: your best
friend, your middle class life, your big house,

a life of adventure and scrapes regarded
with mild disapproval and admiration
by your lawyer father, your fearlessness

in the face of danger, a fearlessness
that belonged nowhere in my Paterson world
where my Italian mother insisted we had to stay

on the cement front stoop. There she knew
we couldn't get into trouble. Through that long
summer, I sat on a wooden chair, my legs resting

on the porch railing, my mind transported
into your world as I followed you
up mountains and into caves. From my porch,

that safe harbor, I could have adventures
without ever having to endure
a sprained ankle or a scraped knee.

Nancy Drew, I still love you
for taking me with you,
carrying me away from the tight

confines of my life, to a place
where everything is possible
and bravery is common

and miraculous as stars.

Last Night My Mother Came Back

Last night my mother came back. I saw her
in the distance, her body draped in wisps of fog,

ethereal as she never was in life, my sturdy
mother, her feet always planted on the ground,

practical and no-nonsense and scolding.
Why doesn't she move toward me

instead of moving away? My sister tells me
my mother visited her in that North Carolina

hospital room, my mother, who never traveled,
who in her life had only been to Italy and New Jersey,

came to my sister. My father came too. My sister
woke up and they were there, sitting in straight-backed

chairs near her bed. They tell my sister to be careful;
then they talk about her children

and the family and what she can do to save herself.
"It was so nice to see them," my sister says. I am hurt

that they do not visit me. When she was dying,
my mother said she couldn't wait until I arrived

every day. My sister, who has always run away
from things she could not face, had to be forced

to visit, but I knew my mother needed me.
I had to be there with her, that swollen belly,

the cancer turning her skin as yellow as a legal pad,
her small hand soft in mine. Now I watch my mother

move away from me, watch her turn, one last time
to look at me, her smile almost a hand on my face,

her love, as always, delivered in gestures
rather than words. I mention her every day,

this woman who taught us to search for grace
in the center of our days.

Laura, Now That You Are Gone

Sometimes I start
To walk across the street,
To your house before I realize
You died more than a month ago.
The plaque you sent me
With its sentimental words
And pink flowers
Hangs in my den.
You must have known
You would die soon.
And wanted me to know
You loved me,
Though we didn't say it
To one another.

Sister, who was so different from me,
Sister, who called for me and I came to you,
Even slept all night in your hospital room
In a hard plastic chair to make sure
You didn't die in the night,
Sister, whose frail, twisted hand
I held in mine,
Sister, who called me on my birthday,
Though you were having trouble breathing,
"Mary, Mary, Where are you?"
And then you sang "Happy Birthday to you,
Happy Birthday to you."

All your energy and desire to live
Caught in your husky, faltering voice

That I hear in my head
When I think of you.

Since Laura Died

Alex, since Laura died, I hear the flat timbre
of your voice, the heaviness in it, the sorrow,

and know that some part of you refuses
to let her go. She held a corner of your world up

for you and without her, a blank space
you don't know how to fill.

Older sister to her baby brother, the roles
played themselves out even after we all grew up,

and you were the doctor and she, your nurse.
In your office she told you what to do,

as she did when we were children
And pretended she was our mother, and we

came to her for help with the American world
Mamma didn't understand. Now I call you,

though I know I can't fill the space where she was,
so many years the surrogate mother, the tie between

the two of you stronger than the one between us.
It was only after she moved to North Carolina

so her daughter could take care of her,
that I realized that you called her every day,

that you paid her $400 a month over her pension,
that just hearing her voice made you feel safe,

and now, with Laura gone and Mom and Dad gone, too,
who will hold the screen between us and

the empty valley where they all vanished, leaving us
alone and trembling in our suburban houses where we don't

know the neighbors and my voice on the phone
isn't enough to comfort you?

The Dodge Silver Hawk

Dennis talks about the Dodge Silver Hawk his father bought
when he was a teenager, a very cool car for a middle-aged
man, light blue and silver. When Dennis shows a picture of it
to his boyhood friend, their eyes light up. Dick says,
"Your father let you drive that car. My father never let me
drive his car. He told me to go out to work to earn the money

to buy my own car." In the old album, the car is parked
in the driveway of the white colonial in River Edge.
It gleams with its sharp edges and polished chrome.
I dated Dick first and met Dennis at Dick's house.
I stopped seeing anyone in the room once Dennis
came in and took out his guitar and sang.

By the time I met Dennis, the Silver Hawk
was only a shining memory, a light in Dennis' eyes
when he talks about it, even now, thirty years later.
When I met him, he was driving a black Pontiac
with dark brown tweed upholstery torn in spots
and a narrow windshield and side windows

with little flaps that opened so you could drive along
and feel the wind on your face. We parked on the Palisades
and looked at the lights of New York across the Hudson,
before we necked and petted and French kissed, until we both
were in a frenzy of unfulfilled lust. He drove me home
with his arm around me. I sat as close to him as I could.

This was the early 1960s and nice Catholic girls did not
go all the way; though my Italian blood was not into
denial of the flesh. If he had asked me,
I would have resisted and then given in
But as a nice Catholic boy, he respected me.
I couldn't break out of the cast of rules that kept me

acting the way I thought I should, afraid of getting pregnant,
of having a policeman shine his light on us, on my
unbuttoned blouse, my unsnapped bra, the heat in my body,
the steamed up windows of his car, the other cars lined up
in a row on that dark lookout.
On our wedding day, my father rented a limousine for us.
After we were married, the photographer asked us to look out

the back window of the limo so he could take our picture.
It is that picture of that I think of first when I think of us,
that girl and boy, so young and unknowing, looking
toward a future they have no way of imagining,
just as I look at the young woman walking toward me,
who has taken her child to the bus and who reminds me

of myself at her age. Perhaps it is the spring in her step
that makes me remember mornings when in half light
we made love before I got dressed to walk the children
to school, my happiness in the way I walked
and the half smile I never could erase from my face.
Today seeing her and remembering, I realize

this is what Dennis and Dick feel when they speak
of the Silver Hawk and the shining they recapture
for a moment before it too vanishes like all time
that passes through our fingers elusive as fog.

Signposts

Today I found an old album with pictures of us,
from 1977, taken on our first trip to Italy.

It is our first trip without our children.
The camera captures us sitting together

at a table with other couples; lifted toward you,
my face so alive and glowing, I might

even be beautiful. I remember finding that I was shy
as I had been as a young girl with all these

strangers who seem foreign to me with their
interest in spending as much money as possible

at each stop of the tour bus. We are not
like them. We feel awkward when they get on the bus

showing off rings, watches, handbags, shoes,
coral pins. We tend to draw together

feeling our difference. We walk. You hold my
hand and our shoulders touch. "Look at the love birds,"

someone says. How right we are for each other, traveling
together in this country of my ancestors, miles

from the mountains where my parents were born, and
as the tour moves toward southern Italy, I start to see faces

that seem familiar, places that look like the places
my mother described when she talked about San Mauro.

The farther South we travel, the more at home I feel,
the dialect familiar and clear. I look back across

all the years between then and now, and see us: you, in your
glasses with heavy black frames, and my face

that couldn't possibly look so untouched, but does.
Pictures, memories. You stand in front of Bernini's

horses in Rome, I, at Pompeii, both of us in a Venetian
gondola where I almost fell into the filthy water

of the Canal. Signposts in our lives. Innocence
palpable, lives yet to move through so much loss.

Geography of Scars

An art that heals and protects itself is a geography of scars.
Wendell Berry

And though I have loved you for more than half my life,
Though we have grown into each other's arms
So that when I am away from you,
I imagine you are with me, our lives,
Gnarled and pitted as the bark of our oak trees,
This illness has moved in with us, a dark presence,
A shadow that hovers behind us as we walk
The path of our days.

I sit in our den with a book in my hands
And hear you call me,
Know by the tone of panic in your voice
That something is wrong.
I find you stuck to the floor,
Help me, you say, and I try.
I push you from behind, touch your foot,
Hold a ruler out in front of you, all the things
That are supposed to help you to move, but don't.

I bring you another pill and then we wait
Until the medicine starts to work
And you are able to walk a few feet to a chair.

I would moan and cry if only it would not hurt you.
Instead I retreat into my book again,
Try not to see the map of our future,
Knowing its lines and angles lead to a place

Where I will trace the geography of my grief,
These scars that remain when you,
Whom I have loved for so long, are gone.

In the New Millennium

In the new millennium, I still will be sitting behind my desk
in the chaos of my office, papers spilling from uneven stacks
around me, sirens sounding outside my windows. The phones
ring so often that a friend I hired to help me tells me
before he quits that the office is like being caught
in the bowels of the Titanic when it is sinking.

In the new millennium I still will be rushing off to poetry
readings and workshops, driving to airports
and down highways.

In the new millennium, you will be waiting for me
when I get home, though last night was the worst night yet,
you unable to move for hours, even the increased medicine
not working, and the new millennium rushing toward us,
only a few weeks left, and maybe then,
when the ball drops in Times Square, maybe it
will bring the magic pill that will cure you so you will be able
to move without help.

In the new millennium, I won't be able to lose any
weight and, at a meeting when I know I shouldn't, I will
stand up and speak out for what I know is right and people
in the room will stare and even my friends will avert their eyes,
though afterwards they will say, "Oh, you have so much
courage. I agreed with you, but I couldn't say it."

In the new millennium I will be exuberantly happy
when I hear my daughter's voice on the phone or when she
rushes down to New Jersey from Boston to see me and I
will lean on her more than I should.

In the new millennium I will be unable to find the
right words to reach my son, our conversations like pushing
a boulder up a mountain.

In the new millennium, Paterson streets will be littered
with the lives of the broken and forgotten, the shuffling men
with wild eyes and the lady in the wheelchair
who rides down the center of the street
in noon-hour traffic and curses anyone
who attempts to help her, even the policeman
whom she hits with her chair.

And in the new millennium, politics will be corrupt and big
money will buy votes, the gap between the rich and the poor
will grow wider, and the rivers more polluted.
In the new millennium, I will see the cup of the world
as half full rather than half empty, beauty even
in the polluted sky, the child reaching up to her mother
in front of city hall and the mother's arms gathering
the child up, her face softening,
her cheek against her child's hair.

When I Leave You

When I leave you in the kitchen doorway, drive
out of the garage with you watching, I realize
how your face grows more and more vulnerable,
worry lines etched in your skin.

Before I left, you said, "Don't worry about me.
I'll be all right. I won't be lonely. Call me
every night," but I don't know how
you will manage.

If I could I would find that old photo of you,
the one of you standing at the dock
in Martha's Vineyard, the white boats
bobbing behind you, John's hand in yours.
John is about two years old; he is wearing
a turquoise sweatshirt and blue jeans,
and you are wearing khaki pants
and a blue windbreaker.

Your face, in its horn-rimmed spectacles,
looks so young, your skin,
clear and glowing, your crewcut
catching and holding the light.
You look strong and healthy,
your shoulders wide inside
the windbreaker, your body, tall
and unbent. I wish I could
superimpose that photo
of your young, healthy self
over the person I am holding now

in my arms who is disappearing.
I would cut you out of that

picture like a paper doll, leave
little flaps to attach to you.
I could pretend that our lives
will go on as we thought they would
that day in Martha's Vineyard
when the world was singing to us
and everything ahead of us
was filled with light . . .

Grief

Grief is a long hallway, a door
That slams shut in the dark
Grief is the hand clamped
On my throat when I watch you
Struggle to move or when I hear
Your feet dragging and tripping
On the kitchen linoleum

The sound of your feet trying
To dislodge themselves
From the places where they
Are inexplicably stuck
The horrible staccato
Of your struggle

I pretend to be deaf
And blind, pretend that you are
The same as your were ten years ago
Five, even one, knowing
We will not go to the theater

Together in our old age
As I thought we would
Or travel together
Knowing that as March vanishes
And April opens its glorious hands
I travel the long road of grief
toward you, my loneliness

Each day deepens, as you move
Away from me, and I
Watch you go, my helpless
Hands hanging at my sides
My mouth calling your name.

These Are Words I Have Said

These are words I have said, over and over.
I count them as if they were carved beads
on the rosary my mother fingered each night,
but my prayers are not strong enough
to stop the hunger
of the disease that each day devours
more of what you once were.

Even your ankles are pitiful,
all bone and stretched flesh,
and your eyes have the stunned look
of birds who have smashed into a window.

Love, I would give you the warmth
of my body, the energy that surges
through me, if only I could.
In my arms now you seem insubstantial.

 I am holding on to you as hard
as I can. I refuse to let you go:
is that the prayer I've been searching for,
the one that will save you?

Poem to My Husband of Thirty-Three Years

Love, I wish I could be angry with you for leaving
when I need you here. You aren't even
leaving all at once: instead you seem
to grow smaller, thinner with each day,

your eyes baffled. You take up less and less space;
I want to hate you for the way you're disappearing.
I have trouble hearing your muted voice
and have to ask you to repeat yourself.

Your walk is so silent, I am often startled
to find you behind me, as though you are
becoming a ghost, parts of you pared away.
Even the air doesn't move when you move.

Sometimes when I come into the house, I call
and call, the house so still I am sure no one is in it,
until you rise up out of your basement room,
after what seems like a long time of shouting

your name, and I grumble, "It's like living
with a dead person." The past, iridescent
and elusive, floats away from us.
I drag the present with me
like a heavy suitcase wherever I go.

Traveler's Advisory

Because there is nowhere to go
Because distance tears
Because I have lived in a big old house
Because I like my little apartment
Because I telephone my husband every night
Because I look out my windows at the lights of Binghamton
Because I can read until late at night without bothering anyone
Because there is something delicious about loneliness
Because loneliness is a choice
Because the third day of each week I feel your need
pulling at me over telephone wires and I say
I'll be home tomorrow and I feel guilty for enjoying
these few months in my own place, suddenly set down
in this new territory without ties:
no husband, children, grandchildren, friends,
only a few people know my phone number
Because the silence of my place is blessed
Because the mountains outside the city are smudges
of charcoal against the gray sky Because by the fourth day
without you the loneliness is greater than my need to be alone
Because on Route 17 barreling toward you in my Honda,
listening to poetry on my car tape player and watching
the road unwinding before me, the evergreens blur
Because, finally, I make the last quick turn
into my driveway and you are waiting.

Water Chestnut

The water chestnut is so perfectly formed,
like a fossil or a flower caught in dark metal,
the tip of it perfect, such attention to detail, grace,

it could be a forsythia leaf carved out of stone
or a bird perhaps, a winged thing. When I turn it
over in my hand, I see that it could be the head

of a steer or a goat. How its forms lend themselves
to conjecture, how impossible to capture as one thing
or another, the way we all are hidden under our skins,

the person on the outside, one thing, and the person
within so different from what appears on the surface,
the way we change as we move through the many facets

of our lives, the way being with someone else changes
the face we present to the world and all the while,
the secret face underneath. The sorrow is like the banging

of a broken muffler or the grief we carry like a cup filled
to the brim, a cup we try to balance in our hands, fearing
that if we were to spill it, if we were to let one drop fall,

we would not be able to stop, the way I could have cried
watching you hitch toward me, your belt pulled one
notch tighter, your leg dragging, the way you said

to my friend , "The second time I saw Maria,
it was at N.Y.U. I saw her ahead of me and she
was rushing. I had to run to catch up to her

and its no different now." I remember that day,
at N.Y.U., when I heard you call my name
and I turned toward you. I could have taken wing

like this water chestnut, I was happy, standing
on that windy February corner, you blond
and young, your shoulders, broad and strong, your face lit.

How to Turn a Phone Call into a Disaster

Sunday morning. Dennis has gone to church;
Because I don't have a workshop or a reading,
I am sitting on the sofa in my nightgown and robe.
I decide to call my son, and first my daughter-in-law
Answers; she sounds surprised that I called.
"Well," she says," I'm just going out. Here's John,"and then,

My son's voice. I ask how the children are, how Caroline
Is managing with her broken arm, and the front door bell rings.
"Oh, who's that?" I say, annoyed but moving to the front door
Holding the phone in my hand. My husband's friend is there,
Saying " Get the walker. Dennis is having trouble."
I get flustered, as I always do in a crisis. "I'll call you back,"

I say, my voice shaking. I rush off to get the walker
With its little wheels, but I can't go outside. I'm still
In my soft slippers and it's raining. I watch Al
And his wife help Dennis up the walk, one on each arm,
Dennis embarrassed and struggling, each step achieved
After immense effort. Panic fills my chest like hundreds

Of mosquitoes. In the hall, the carpet catches in Dennis' feet,
And I shout "Stop, stop, you have to lift your feet," as though
He can help having his feet stuck to the floor. His body leans
Toward the walker as it slides away from him, his torso
Parallel with the floor. I lean over to pull his feet forward;
Only later do I realize that my fat thighs must have been
    visible
When I bent down. I get a chair for him; thank Al and his wife,
get Dennis a glass of water and his pills, my hands distraught

So I know I could never be a nurse or a doctor and I think

How terrible I am at this, and what a bad caretaker I'll make,

"What will I do? How will I manage?" I leave Dennis

Sitting in a chair in the living room waiting for his medicine

To work, and I go into the den to call John back. Before I get
     past,

"Hello," I hear Dennis calling me, his voice tremulous.
     "Wait, John,

I have to see what he wants," and with the phone in my hand,

I run out to the living room where Dennis goes through an
     elaborate

And slow explanation of how he wants me to ask John
     whether he uses

An electric razor and does it work and what kind does he use.

His friend told him that he uses a Norelco. What does John
     think?

It takes him ten minutes to say all this, as my mother-in-law

Used to say "To make a long story short," and she'd go on
     for two hours,

So when he keeps on explaining what I already understand,
     nervous

Laughter starts to bubble up into my chest. I rush back into
     the other room

And explain to John about the razor, and suddenly, I am
     sobbing and can't

Stop. I only cried like this, without restraint, maybe four
     times in my life,

But I can't stop and I can't get words out while my son is
     saying,

"Mom, what's the matter? What's the matter?" When I can
     speak again,
I say, "John, you needed this phone call like you needed a hole
In your head!" I've added one more worry to this son of
     mine who takes
Responsibility on his shoulders like an old man, though he is
     only thirty-four,
I try to make small talk, ask about his job, the children, the
     new house.
I can feel my composure crumbling, my voice starting to
     break apart again.
I think I could make a million dollars teaching people how
     to ruin
A person's day with a phone call.

This Morning

When the alarm goes off at 4:30, I leap out of bed
so I won't wake you and then I realize

you are already awake, your eyes staring
into darkness, your voice reedy and thin. You ask for a drink

of water and an Advil, and when I carry them to you, I see
that you are trembling, your eyes frightened.

"What is going to happen to me?" you ask.
I try to soothe you, try to find the words that will lull

you back onto the smooth lake of sleep, but the words
are fragile as paper boats. They cannot stay afloat.

I have to rush off, leaving you behind so I can be
in East Brunswick at 7 a.m., after driving

through the most congested areas in New Jersey,
cars snaking in a line ahead of me even this early.

Guilt washes over me for having chosen this life that takes
me away from you, while you lie in bed looking

like a slender child who needs to be held
and comforted. It is this image of you that I carry

as I drive down the Parkway And onto the New Jersey
Turnpike and onto Cranbury Road and into the high school

and into the classes where I read a poem about you
because a student asks me to. I tell them

about you, the image I cannot wash out of my head,
even though I know it is too sad for them. My mother

always said "Young people shouldn't be told about
the troubles of adults. They'll have enough troubles

soon themselves." Their eyes say it's ok,
and they come up to talk to me. One young man

hands me a poem he wrote, others seem to need
to touch my arm or hand, and I am comforted

as I have not been comforted before.

Shame

Today I was thinking about shame and how much
it is a part of everything we do, about the way
I was ashamed at ten to say to my cousin
that my mother asked me to buy toilet paper,

as though my grown-up male cousin didn't use
toilet paper and wasn't stuck with all those messy bodily
functions we have to plan our lives around, the way public
bathrooms and our need for them remind us of our humanity,

a cosmic joke on us, so we won't forget how rooted we are
to the earth and not the ethereal beings the nuns wanted us
to be. Today I was thinking about shame and I see Dennis,
thin and frail and naked, the skin stretched tight over

his big bones, not an ounce of fat to cover him, the skin blue
and translucent, as he crawls from the bedroom on his
helpless legs to the bathroom. How ashamed he is,
as though this illness were a failure of his own manhood

and he to blame, how he pounds his fists on the floor in
frustration,how he scuttles into the bathroom and closes
the door after I see the dark well of sorrow in his eyes.
Today I am thinking about shame, and wish

it were only toilet paper or a red splotch on my dress
or my inability to learn the Periodic Table in Chemistry
that made me feel it, instead of my convoluted feelings
about my husband's illness, how nothing in our lives

is all one thing or another, not love, not grief, not anger,
but always mixed with its opposite emotion. I see Dennis
crawling along the floor, and I am struck with the axe of grief,
a terrible pity that can do no good, but mixed in with it,

the shame of my own impatience when he can't
remember something I told him two minutes ago,
or when he struggles for twenty minutes to open a package
and won't accept help, or when he insists he can walk

down the stairs and falls, the corrosive shame of my quick
annoyance, the shame of my lack of patience,
the shame of feeling that his illness is a deep
and muddy river in which we both will drown.

Donna Laura

Donna Laura, they called my grandmother
when they saw her sitting in the doorway, sewing
delicate tablecloths and linens, hours of sewing
bent over the cloth, an occupation for a lady.

Donna Laura, with her big house falling
to ruins around her head,
Donna Laura, whose husband
left for Argentina when she was twenty-four,
left her with seven children and no money
and her life in that southern Italian village
where the old ladies watched her
from their windows. She could not have
taken a breath without everyone knowing

Donna Laura who each day sucked
on the bitter seed
of her husband's failure
to send money and to remember
her long auburn hair,

Donna Laura who relied on the kindness
of the priest's "housekeeper"
to provide food for her family.
Everyone in the village knew

my grandmother's fine needlework
could not support seven children,
but everyone pretended not to see.

When she was ninety, Donna Laura
still lived in that mountain house.

Was her heart a bitter raisin,
her anger so deep it could have cut
a road through the mountain?
I touch the tablecloth she made,

the delicate scrollwork,
try to reach back to Donna Laura,
feel her life shaping itself into laced patterns
and scalloped edges from all those years between
her young womanhood and old age.

Only this cloth remains,
old and perfect still, turning her bitterness into art
to teach her granddaughters and great granddaughters
how to spin sorrow into gold.

Learning How to Love Myself

My hair is dark black and electric. Left to itself
it would spring off my head in ringlets. I could never

control it, not when I was growing up. It stuck out
from my head like a kinky tent. My legs are stumpy

and thick, the knees swollen, the veins protruding.
My small feet are wide and my body is planted

on the ground like a fat shrub. When I sit
on a high stool in the TV station, I see my short,

sturdy legs, my thick body that carries me along,
unstoppable into my life, this peasant body.

For years, I longed for the slender grace
of a long body, tall and supple as marsh grass,

but would not give up this incredible energy,
the heat that pours from the furnace of my body,

the long line of women who taught me to laugh
my deep belly laugh and grab the world

in my arms and squeeze the sweetness out.

Maria Mazziotti Gillan is the Executive Director of the Poetry Center at Passaic County Community College and the Director of the Creative Writing Program at Binghamton University, SUNY. She is also the editor of *The Paterson Literary Review.* With her daughter Jennifer Gillan, she edited *Unsettling America: An Anthology of Contemporary Multicultural Poetry* (Viking/Penguin), *Identity Lessons: Contemporary Writing about Learning to be American* (Penguin/Putnam), and *Growing Up Ethnic in America* (Penguin/Putnam). She is the author of seven books of poetry, the most recent being *Where I Come From: Selected and New Poems* (Guernica, 1995) and *Things My Mother Told Me* (Guernica, 1999).

AGMV Marquis

MEMBER OF SCABRINI MEDIA

Quebec, Canada